African People in World History

African People in World History

by

John Henrik Clarke

A BCP Contemporary Lecture

Black Classic Press P.O. Box 13414 Baltimore, MD 21203

African People in World History

Library of Congress Catalog Card Number: 90-82687
ISBN-13 978-0-933121-77-5
ISBN-10 0-933121-77-6
Cover design and art by Sean Ramõn Montague

Printed on acid free paper to assure long life

Founded in 1978, Black Classic Press specializes in bringing to light obscure and significant works by and about people of African descent. If our books are not available in your area, ask your local bookseller to order them. Our current list of titles can be obtained by writing:

Black Classic Press
c/o List
P.O. Box 13414
Baltimore, MD 21203-3414
A Young Press With Some Very Old Ideas

Dedication

To the three men who have had the greatest influence on my life and career as a student and eventually as a teacher of history:

Arthur A. Schomburg,
who taught me how to understand the interrelationship of African history to world history;

Willis N. Huggins,
founder and director of the Harlem History Club of the 1930s, who taught me how to understand the political meaning of history;

William Leo Hansberry,
whose lectures, articles, and extensive writings on the subject taught me the philosophical meaning of African history and world history in general.

Illustrations

Contents

Introduction

The history of Africans in the Americas and in the Caribbean Islands is incomplete without an examination of the African past. This background is indispensable to an intelligent approach to African American history. As a teacher of the subject I have taught that history is a clock that people use to tell their political and cultural time of day. It is also a compass that people use to find themselves on the map of human geography.

History tells a people where they have been and what they have been, where they are and what they are. Most important, an understanding of history tells a people where they still must go and what they still must be.

Until quite recently, it was rather generally assumed, even among well-educated persons in the West, that the African continent was a great expanse of land, mostly jungle, inhabited by savages and fierce beasts. It was not thought of as an area where great civilizations could have existed or where the great kings of these civilizations could have ruled in might and wisdom over vast empires.

Although the cultural achievements of Egypt were acknowledged, Egypt was conceived of as European rather than African. Even if a look at an atlas or globe showed Egypt to be in Africa, the Sahara represented a formidable barrier and a convenient division of Africa into two parts: one, north of the Sahara, inhabited by European-like people of high culture and noble history, the other, south of the Sahara, inhabited by dark-skinned people who had no culture, were incompetent, and had done nothing in their dark and distant past that could be dignified as "history."

"Although the cultural achievements of Egypt were acknowledged, Egypt was conceived of as European rather than African."

If Africa in general is a man-made mystery, Egypt in particular is a bigger one. For generations, European "scholars" have attempted to deny that Egypt was a part of Africa. Such ideas, of course, are far from the truth, as we shall see. But it is not difficult to understand why they persisted and, unfortunately, still persist in the public mind.

Western scholars have acknowledged only recently that the Nile River, which is four thousand miles long, starts in the south, in the heart of Africa, and flows to the north. It was the world's first cultural highway. Thus, ancient Egypt was a composite of many African cultures. Bruce Williams implies in *The Lost Pharaohs of Nubia,* that the nations to Egypt's south could be older than Egypt. This information is not new. When rebel

European scholars were saying this one hundred years ago and proving it, they were not taken seriously.

Herodotus, the Greek historian who travelled in Africa about 450 B.C., could still see evidence of greatness in the Nile Valley, although it was partly in ruins after many invasions. By that time, the Nile Valley civilization of Africa had already brought forth two Golden Ages of achievement and had left its mark for all the world to see.

In *The African Origin of Civilization: Myth or Reality,* Cheikh Anta Diop, the African historian, has said, in effect, that the history of Africa would be out of kilter unless the relationship of Egypt to the rest of Africa is in proper focus. In *The Destruction of Black Civilization,* Chancellor Williams entitled his second chapter, "Ethiopia's Oldest Daughter: Egypt." In summarizing the history of the people that the Greeks later called "Egyptians," Chancellor Williams explained the circumstances of their migration from the Upper to the Lower Nile River.

Further evidence of the southern African origins of the Egyptians has been supplied by Yosef ben-Jochannan in *Abu Simbel to Ghizeh: A Guide Book and Manual,* and *Black Man of the Nile and His Family.* In *Abu Simbel to Ghizeh,* ben-Jochannan says:

> This Guide Book or Manual, will concentrate on those many aspects which depicted the indigenous African contributions to the

High-Culture of TA-Merry-Nubia that reached its first zenith before the original foreign invaders of Africa called "Hyksos" or "Shepherd Kings of Bedunia," in ca. 1675 B.C.E., XIIIth Dynasty, conquered the Delta Region of Egypt, Northeast Africa.

It is unfortunate that so much of the history of Africa has been written by conquerors, missionaries, and adventurers. Fortunately, the Egyptians left the best record of their own history. It was not until near the end of the eighteenth century, when a few European scholars learned to decipher their writing, that this was understood. For example, the highly respected "Papyrus of Hunefer," in the Egyptian's *Book of the Coming Forth by Day and Night,* documented the southern African origin of the ancient Egyptians. "We came from the beginning of the Nile where God Hapi dwells, at the foothills of the mountain of the moon. Kilimanjaro between Kenya and Tanzania, or Rwenzori in Uganda."

"It is unfortunate that so much of the history of Africa has been written by conquerors, missionaries, and adventurers."

The Nile Valley's first age of high cultural grandeur lasted until the eve of the Christian era. Some aspects of it survived the Greek and Roman occupation of parts of North Africa. After the rise and decline of Greek civilization and the Roman destruction of the city of Carthage, the Romans organized the conquered territories into a province they called Africa, a word derived from "afri," the name of a group of people about whom little is known. This was a new name because previously all

14

dark-skinned people were called "Ethiopians," since the Greeks referred to Africa as "Ethiopia—the land of the burnt-face people."

After 300 A.D., new states and eventually empires began to appear in inner West Africa, which the Arabs later called the Western Sudan. The best known of these states were Ghana, Mali, and Songhay. Their collective life span was more than a thousand years, but these West African empires were in decline on the eve of the slave trade.

In most Western textbooks, the history of Africa and its people is approached as if Africans had no history worth recording before the Europeans contacted them. This one-dimensional approach to African history generally starts with slavery and infers that African people are the only people who have ever been slaves. Slavery is an old institution. In one way or the other, and at different times, slavery has touched the life of nearly every ethnic group on the face of the earth. However, the form of slavery that the Arabs introduced into East Africa, and the Europeans introduced into the states of West Africa, had never existed in Africa or the world before. This system of slavery led to a massive depopulation of Africa and the wreck and ruin of a large number of African societies.

As a rationale for the slave trade and the colonial system that followed it, Europeans had to forget, or pretend to forget, all they had previously known about African history, African people, and their culture. Historian and political activist, Richard B. Moore, observed in "The Significance of African History," one of his last articles, that:

> The significance of African history is shown, though not overtly, in the very effort to deny anything worthy of the name of history to Africa and the African peoples. This widespread, and well nigh successful endeavor, maintained through some five centuries, to erase African history from the general record, is a fact which of itself should be quite conclusive to thinking and open minds. For it is logical and apparent that no such understanding should ever have been carried on, and at such length, in order to obscure and bury what is actually of little or no significance.

"Mr. Moore is saying, in essence, that African history must be looked at anew and seen in its relationship to world history."

Moore's observation becomes even more discerning when one realizes that this deliberate denial of African history followed the European invasion of Africa in the middle of the fifteenth century. Europeans felt a compulsion thereafter to justify such conquests, plunder, and enslavement. A brash denial of African history, culture, and, indeed, even of human qualities and capacity for civilization was *fostered*. Mr. Moore is saying, in essence, that African history must be looked at anew and seen in its relationship to world history. First, the distortions must be admitted. The hard fact is that most of what we now call world history is only the history of the first and second rise of Europe. The Europeans are not yet

16

willing to acknowledge that the world did not wait in darkness for them to bring the light. The history of Africa was already old when Europe was born.

It is too often forgotten that more than five thousand years had unfolded before what was to become Europe was a political factor in world affairs. When the early Europeans first met Africans at the crossroads of history, it was a respectful meeting, and the Africans were not slaves. Their nations were old before Europe was born. In this period of history, what was to be later known as "Africa" was an unknown place to the people who would someday be called "Europeans." Only the people of some of the Mediterranean Islands and of a few Greek and Roman states knew of parts of North Africa, which was a land of mystery to them.

"When the early Europeans first met Africans at the crossroads of history, it was a respectful meeting, and the Africans were not slaves."

The Atlantic slave trade and the rationale used to justify it locked African history into what Ivan Van Sertima has called, "the five-hundred-year room." For five hundred years, the history of African people has been mainly interpreted by non-Africans who had their own interest at heart. The story of Africa before the trans-Atlantic slave trade is generally unknown. Slavery is only one factor in African history and it, too, is misunderstood.

African history as world history

When we think of scientific research on early man in Africa, the name of the famed British archaeologist, Louis S. B. Leakey, comes immediately to mind. Single-handedly, this dedicated specialist, who spent nearly a lifetime in the Olduvai Gorge, the "Grand Canyon" of South East Africa, changed our entire concept of the age of the first man. He identified the bones of a man at least two million years old. Thus, it would seem that Africa was the birthplace of man. But this great continent was not only the birthplace of man, its peoples created early civilizations that were in the forefront of world progress: the cultures of Egypt, Kush, and Ethiopia.

At Olduvai Gorge in the same general area where the fossils of the earliest man were discovered, Leakey made another discovery, which he called *homo habilis,* or "house-dwelling man." *Homo habilis* was even more advanced than his previous find having been dated scientifically at about two million years.

Early man in Africa made use of pebble tools. They had no well-defined shape, but a few flakes were removed irregularly to give a sharp edge. Early pebble tools have been found in several sites in South Africa, at Olduvai Gorge and at a few other sites in East Africa. Evidence of pebble tools has also been found in Portugal and in southwestern Asia, indicating that for a period of a million and a half years, man, the pebble toolmaker, wandered across much of Africa, into and probably through southern Asia, and occasionally into Europe across a land bridge that existed at the time. This land bridge was probably somewhere near what is now the Strait of Gibraltar.

During the dawn of history, Africans worked out and solved some of the basic problems of surviving in changing climatic conditions and hostile environments. From about thirty to one hundred thousand years ago, the discovery of fire, the invention of the handle and other two-piece tools, the beginning of travel by water, as well as fishing, rapidly changed and improved human existence. During this period known as the Old Stone Age, men and women lived a very simple life and used the environment around them. They learned how to make tools to kill animals; they discovered how to start a fire. They used the skins of the beasts they killed to keep themselves warm. Drawings of animal bones, hearts, and other organs from the Old Stone Age still exist. These early drawings are part of man's early beginnings in the field of anatomy and illustrative art.

Another great leap forward in human progress occurred when early man in Africa started to polish his tools. In polishing his tools, man had discovered something that would influence his total existence for all time to come—he had become aware of beauty. He would soon make paint and decorate his surroundings. In mixing one substance with another to create paint, he had, unbeknown to himself, begun the basis for the science of chemistry.

The New Stone Age started when man domesticated plants and animals. Man learned how to take wild seeds and plant them so he could grow his own food. This was the beginning of farming. Now families could stay in one place for a long time, because there was enough food to eat. Stock raising further helped to stabilize the early African community. When the villager could raise his own meat supply, less hunting was necessary. More time was then devoted to developing the community and its resources. Domesticating plants and animals was an advancement almost as essential as the use of fire. With this new stability, villages began to develop into cities.

The importance of family as a social unit in the development of man has remained unchanged down through the years. The first human societies were developed to meet the survival needs of the family. The early Africans had to find a way to communicate with those around them and to create the village that became the city, and subsequently the state. Early man had to make hooks for fishing, spears for hunting, and knives for cutting. The inventive mind of early man was prodded by the needs of his family that required him to search for new ways of gathering and raising food, domesticating animals, and building shelter such as the thatched hut, which was the first man-made home. The early Africans also discovered basketmaking and weaving.

By this time, Africa had benefited from the introduction of iron, agriculture, animal husbandry, and the use of irrigation. Europe was not yet a factor in developing cultures and civilizations when these groundbreaking events in Africa were contributing to the beginnings of organized societies.

The distorters of African history have chosen to ignore the fact that the people of the ancient land, which would later be called Egypt, never called their country by that name. It was called Ta-Merry and sometimes Kemet or Sais. The ancient Hebrews called it Mizrain. Both the Greeks and the Romans referred to the country as, The "Pearl of the Nile." The Greeks gave it the simple name *Aegyptcus*. Thus, the name *Egypt* is of Greek origin.

The ancient Egyptians were distinctly African people. They were not Hamites, as some history books tend to indicate. The manners and customs and religions of the historic Egyptians suggest that the original home of their prehistoric ancestors was south in a country in the neighborhood of Uganda and Punt. (The Biblical land of Punt is believed to be in the area now known as Somalia.)

In many ways, Egypt is the key to ancient African history. Unless Egypt is seen as an African nation, African history becomes distorted. The invasions of Egypt that started about 1675 B.C. and continued until after the Roman period brought into Egypt large numbers of people who were not indigenous to the country. The bulk of the Arab population in present-day Egypt has no direct relationship to ancient Egyptian history. Most of them came into Africa in the seventh and eighth centuries during the rapid spread of Islam.

The famous inscription found in the Temple of Horus at Edfu and known as the *Edfu Text* is an important source document on the early history of the Nile Valley. This text gives an account of the origin of Egyptian civilization. According to this record, civilization was brought from the south by a band of wanderers under the leadership of King Horus, who was later deified. His followers were called "the black-smiths" because they possessed iron implements. This early culture has been traced back to Somalia, although it may have originated in the Great Lakes region of Central Africa.

In Somalia and present-day Zimbabwe, there are ruins of buildings constructed with dressed stone and showing a close resemblance to the architecture of early Egypt. Many inventions, such as pyramid building, which we think of as Egyptian inventions, have their origins in the nations south of Egypt. The Nile River played a major role in the relationship of Egypt to the nations in southeast Africa. As a great cultural highway, the Nile River brought elements of civilization into inner Africa during ancient times. If Egypt can be credited with creating the world's first civilization, that credit must be shared with people in other parts of Africa.

No individual in ancient Egypt left a deeper impression than the commoner, Imhotep. He was probably the world's first multigenius and the real father of medicine. Imhotep, the Wise, as he was called, was the Grand Vizier and Court Physician to King Zoser. He was also the architect of the Great Pyramid. He became a deity and later a universal god of medicine whose image graced the first Temple of Imhotep, mankind's first hospital. Sufferers from all over the world came to the temple for prayer, peace, and healing. Imhotep lived in the court of King Zoser where he established his reputation as a healer in the third dynasty about 2980 B.C. One of his best-known sayings, one that is still being quoted, is, "Eat, drink, and be merry, for tomorrow we shall die."

When significant elements of Egyptian civilization were transferred and became the foundation of what we think of as Greek culture, the teachings of Imhotep were absorbed along with the teachings of other great African teachers. When Greek civilization became predominant in the Mediterranean area, the Greeks wanted the world to think that they were the originators of everything. They stopped acknowledging their early debt to Imhotep and other great Africans. Imhotep was forgotten for thousands of years and Hippocrates, a legendary figure of some two thousand years, later became known as the father of medicine. In spite of the neglect and misinterpretation of that day and later achievements, the intellectual aspect of Egypt's Golden Age started with Imhotep. The dynasties from the third through the sixth can be called the building dynasties and from the sixth through the thirteenth were the dynasties of consolidation. North Africa and the Nile Valley nations extending to the south were invaded in 1675 B.C. for the very first time. The Hebrew entry into Africa occurred in 1700 B.C. The Seventeenth and Eighteenth Dynasties were occupied in driving out the invaders with help from Egypt's relatives in the south. This established the greatness of the Eighteenth Dynasty. Out of this dynasty came a family named Thotmoses or Thutmose. One of the first great female rulers in history came out of this dynasty. Her name was Hatshepsut. She was opposed by her brother, Thotmose III, and his supporters. During this period of conflict, Thotmose III learned the basics of power and how to handle it exceptionally well, thanks to the prodding of his sister. After her death, he became one of Egypt's greatest pharaohs.

In 1300 B.C., a sickly boy, whose name was Amenhotep IV, came to power and took the name Akhneton. He was a social reformer, a pacifist, and one of the first men to announce the concept of monotheism. He has been referred to as the "Heretic King." Near the end of this dynasty a young teenager, Tutankhamon, came to power. Some historians have cruelly referred to him as a minor king who had a major funeral. He is commonly known as King Tut.

The Eighteenth Dynasty was followed by a dynasty often called the Ramses dynasty because of the illustrious career of Ramses II and his beautiful Nubian wife, Nefertari, who came from what is now the Sudan. The next five dynasties are sometimes referred to as holding dynasties. Egypt and the Nile Valley civilization neither moved forward nor backward. This stagnation made possible a military dynasty coming from the south, starting in 751 B.C. and lasting approximately 110 years. This dynasty has been called the Ethiopian or Nubian dynasty. When at last it was pushed out of Egypt and had to retreat to its southern homeland, Egypt's Golden Age ended.

Invaders from outside of Africa came again. First the Assyrians, now known as the Syrians, came in 666 B.C. Next the Persians, now known as Iranians, came in 550 B.C. The first purely European invasion of Africa occurred in 332 B.C. under the leadership of a young Macedonian known in history as Alexander the Great.

The weakening and the decline of Greek influence increased Roman designs on North Africa, especially the commercial city of Carthage. This was the basis of the Punic Wars. After holding Rome at bay for nearly 20 years, Hannibal, the North African general, was defeated, and large parts of North Africa became the headquarters of the Eastern Roman Empire. At that time, North Africa was the breadbasket of the Roman empire. This Roman Empire lasted in some form for nearly seven hundred years during which Africa played a major role in both the political as well as the Holy Roman Empire.

Africa and the Roman Empire

By today's social standards, the Romans would be considered very snobbish, but they did not practice racial and national prejudice as it is known today. Consequently, Africans played significant roles in both the

27

political and Holy Roman empire. Septimius Severus, for example, the most noted of the African emperors of Rome, was also the Roman representative to England, where he died at York.

The Romans started a number of important things in Africa and ended an equal number. As conquerors, they did the things that conquerors do: they ruled. Their standard of tax collection would later influence the whole world. The last flickering flame of Nile Valley civilization ended during the Roman occupation of Egypt. The often told story of Cleopatra and her relationship with Julius Caesar and Mark Anthony came out of the Roman-African period.

"The last flickering flame of Nile Valley civilization ended during the Roman occupation of Egypt."

When Alexander of Macedonia married many of his army generals into Egyptian royalty, he created the basis for Cleopatra's family still to come. She was of mixed Greek and Persian ancestry. If she lived today in the United States, she would probably be classified as a light-skinned African American. She was born in 69 B.C. on the eve of the Christian era. She was the seventh person to bear the name Cleopatra. She was an absolute ruler who tried to save Egypt from the worst aspect of Roman domination. She had African loyalties and political might, and by today's standard, she would be considered an African Nationalist. She was the last ruler of Egyptian birth and part African ancestry to rule

Egypt before the emergence of Gamal Abdul Nasser some two thousand years later.

It is often forgotten that Christianity rose at a time when the heavy hand of Rome held sway over large areas of North Africa and Western Asia, and that the Christian story is to a great extent an African story. While the Romans were killing Christians in their arenas, they were also killing African Christians, sometimes in larger numbers, in the amphitheaters of the Roman-dominated areas of North Africa, mainly in the area known as Tunisia. Internal disputes between different sections of the Roman Empire and the mismanagement of Christianity by the Romans led to another era of dissatisfaction. This in turn opened the door to the rise of Islam.

Africa and the rise of Islam

The first seven centuries after the birth of Christ was a troubled period in most of Africa. In North Africa, it was the period of Greek domination, then Roman domination, and a period of occasional difficulties with the people in Western Asia, now called the Middle East. The fall of the Roman empire created a political vacuum in North Africa and parts of Western Asia. African and Asian displeasure at the manipulation of the Christian church opened the door for the emergence of Islam. Islam had a military and a cultural arm. It swept across North Africa with little difficulty and was soon making inroads into mainland Asia. It spread into West Africa, the part the Arabs referred to as the Western Sudan.

According to tradition, Hadzraat Bilal ibn Rahab, a tall, gaunt, bush-haired, indigenous Ethiopian, was the first convert to Islam after Mohamet himself. Bilal was the first muezzin and later became the first high priest and treasurer of the Islamic empire, which today numbers almost three hundred million adherents. Bilal was one of many Africans who helped establish Islam and later made proud names for themselves in the Islamic wars of expansion.

Among African chiefs who converted to the Islamic faith during the Arab invasion of Morocco was a great general known as Gilbril Tarik. Tarik was a general in the Arab-Moorish armies of Musa-ibn-Nusair. Musa later left General Tarik in charge of Tangiers and made him governor of Mauritania.

Tarik, now governor of Mauritania, entered into friendly relations with Count Julian, governor of Ceuta, who was on very bad terms with his master, Roderic, the King of Spain. Count Julian urged Tarik to invade Spain. Thus, in 711 AD, General Tarik, accompanied by one hundred horses and four hundred African soldiers, crossed over into Spain on an exploratory mission. Tarik's small army ravaged several Spanish towns and returned to Africa laden with spoils. Later the same year, he sailed again for Spain in command of an army of seven thousand Africans. Tarik crossed from Africa to Gibraltar (originally named for him in Arabic, Gibrilal-Tarik, that is, Tarik's mountain). Tarik defeated King Roderic the same year in the battle of Gaudalete. He sent for reinforcements from Africa and conquered most of the Iberian Peninsula. Thus began the Moorish rule of Spain that did not end until 1492. Stanley Lane-Poole's *The Story of the Moors in Spain* is an excellent chronicle of this period.

"The Moors built magnificent cities in Spain. The streets were paved, and there were sidewalks for pedestrians."

The Moors built magnificent cities in Spain. Cordoba in the tenth century was much like a modern metropolis. The streets were paved, and there were sidewalks for pedestrians. At night, it was said, "One could travel for ten miles by the light of lamps along an uninterrupted extent of buildings." This was several hundred years before there was a paved street in Paris or a street lamp in London. The population of the city was over one million. There were twenty thousand homes, eight hundred public schools, many colleges and universities, and over one thousand palaces besides the many royal palaces surrounded by beautiful gardens.

31

The mighty kingdoms of Ghana, Mali, and Songhay

Africans were great makers of culture long before their first appearance in Jamestown, Virginia in 1619. Moreover, the rich and colorful history, art, and folklore of West Africa—the ancestral home of most African Americans—present evidence of this, and more. Contrary to a misconception that still prevails, Africans were familiar with literature and art for many years before their contact with the Western world.

Before the disintegration of the political structures of the West African states of Ghana, Mali, and Songhay and the consequent internal strife and chaos that made the slave trade possible, the forefathers of the Africans who eventually became slaves in the United States lived in a society where university life existed and scholars were held in reverence. In this ancestry, there were rulers who expanded their kingdoms into empires and built great and magnificent armies whose numbers coerced entire nations into submission. There were generals who advanced the technique of military science, scholars whose vision of life showed foresight and wisdom, and priests who spoke of gods that were strong and kind. The old state or empire of Ghana was the first of the great kingdoms of the Western Sudan (West Africa) to become known to

Europe. According to one account, the kingdom of Ghana began in the second century A.D. and had a known history of one thousand years. However, some writers believe that Ghana was founded as early as 700 B.C. since an impressive list of 44 kings had ruled in that land before 1000 A.D.

Near the end of the eighth century (770 A.D.), a dynasty of indigenous African kings came to power. Some of the previous kings came from Wagudugu. These were Mossi people who came from an area formerly called, Upper Volta, and is now called Burkina Faso. The indigenous kings were called Sarakoles or Sonikes. The time from the beginning of this dynasty to the invasion of Ghana by Abu Bekr of the Sosso in 1076 A.D. was the Golden Age of ancient Ghana.

Ghana was a well-organized state with a centralized government when the Arabs first mentioned it in 800 A.D. The capital was Kumbisaleh, a large city with stone houses of many stories. The Arab merchants related that in those days the borders of Ghana reached the Atlantic and stretched eastward as far as Timbuktu. After absorbing several small kingdoms in the south, the rulers of Ghana founded the city of Djenne and built it into one of the most prosperous centers of the Western Sudan. The city of Djenne became a great center of learning long before the building of the great University of Sankore at Timbuktu.

The Arab writer El-Bekri states: "The army of Ghana consisted of two hundred thousand warriors, of whom forty thousand were archers." The capital city was highly prosperous, and many of the houses were built of stone. Large numbers of inhabitants wore clothing of silk and velvet. Jewels and weapons of gold and silver were not uncommon. Lawyers and scholars were much respected. Ghana, at this time in her history, was the great gold-producing center of the Western Sudan. The gold and prosperity of Ghana made this nation a prize worthy of conquest. The king of the Sosso Empire invaded Ghana with 50,000 soldiers but was unable to take the country. Ghana was invaded again in the year 1020 A.D. by another army allied with a fanatical Muslim sect called the Almoravids. In the year 1060 A.D., the emperor of Morocco, hoping to capture the rich gold mines, sent another army to invade Ghana. In 1060 A.D., the last and the greatest king of ancient Ghana's golden age came to power. His name was Tenkamenin. He stabilized the country and held off all invaders until 1076 A.D.

The Arab writer El-Bekri states: "The army of Ghana consisted of two hundred thousand warriors, of whom forty thousand were archers."

An Arab geographer, Ibn Haukal, wrote a book about old Ghana in 700 A.D. He described the court of the king of Ghana as a place with sculpture, frescoes, and windows of crystal. He said that horses slept on carpets in the royal stables, and the king sat on a throne of pure gold.

Agriculture was highly developed, and its gold mines were famous. The wealth of the country was spoken of as far away as Baghdad.

The year 770 A.D. was a turning point in the history of old Ghana. A new dynasty of indigenous kings came to power. The country had been ruled by kings who came from another part of Africa. The new royal house expanded the territory of the country and started a period of trade and prosperity. The Soninke Dynasty made the country strong and rich, but the richness of old Ghana was a mixed blessing as she felt the increasing pressure of rising Muslim military power. The threat from the states in the north continued to increase until at last a hostile and determined army invaded the soil of Ghana in 1020 A.D.

The Muslims of northern Ghana never forgave the royal family for preventing the spread of Islam throughout Ghana in the ninth and tenth centuries. In one of their numerous holy wars in 1076 A.D., they united in a campaign under the leadership of Mansa Abu Bekr of the Sosso Empire to overthrow the reigning dynasty of Ghana. The conquest of Ghana brought its Golden Age to an end, but the character of the country was slow to change. Nearly a hundred years later the writer, El Idrisi, spoke of it as "the greatest kingdom of the Blacks." He mentions that the country was ruled by a king of Berber descent who governs by his own authority, but gives allegiance to the Abbasside Sultan of Egypt. The people still had not become Muslims.

In a later account, El Idrisi said, "Ghana. . .is the most considerable, the most thickly populated and the most commercial of the Black countries. It is visited by rich merchants from all the surrounding countries and from the extremities of the West."

"Three great rulers, Sundiata (1230-1255 A.D.), Sukura (1285-1300 A.D.) and Mansa Musa (1306-1332 A.D.) made Mali one of the great empires of West Africa during the thirteenth and fourteenth centuries."

In the year 1087, the people of Ghana were able to throw off the yoke of Sosso and recover their independence, but the country was never the same again. The old unity and grandeur were not recovered. The province of Ghana became a part of the Mali Empire and was later absorbed into the empire of Songhay. Thus, old Ghana, the first great empire of the Western Sudan passed into memory.

Mali, the second of the great empires of Western Sudan, rose up against great odds, and absorbed the territory that once was ancient Ghana after defending itself from another invasion by the Sosso people of what is now Senegal and Mauritania. Three great rulers, Sundiata (1230-1255 A.D.), Sukura (1285-1300 A.D.) and Mansa Musa (1306-1332 A.D.) made Mali one of the great empires of West Africa during the thirteenth and fourteenth centuries.

The origins and early history of the Mali empire are enshrouded in the myths that obscure the earlier periods of African history, but the main outlines of its story and the names and the events of the reigns of most of its kings are rather well known for the period between the middle of the eleventh and the end of the sixteenth centuries. The royal family that presided over this great empire in earlier times still exists. The deposed president of the Mali Republic, Modibo Keita, is a direct descendant of Sundiata Keita, founder of the Mali Empire.

In *Negroes of Africa,* the French historian, Maurice Delafosse, observed that "after a known history of more than thirteen hundred years, the royal family of Mali is probably the most ancient dynasty that is still in power." According to the folk tradition of this country, a king of Mali, named Baramendana, was converted to Islam in the year 1050 A.D. Tradition also states that prior to his conversion, the country had experienced a great and prolonged drought. It is said that he was advised by a Muslim named Omar to accept Islam so that the blessing of rain would once more be visited upon his country. Baramendana accepted the new religion, and his country was blessed with abundant rainfall.

Baramendana entered into relations with neighboring states and enhanced the growth, power, and development of his country. By now, he no longer considered himself a vassal of the empire of Ghana. The city of Timbuktu, by tradition, is said to have been founded as a market and meeting place for the people of the Sudan and western Sahara sometime during this period.

After the death of Baramendana, there are a number of missing pages in the history of Mali. The country grew weak during the twelfth century but was literally reborn during the reign of Sundiata. Sundiata was the greatest king of Mali and is still its national hero. In the year 1224 A.D., the kingdom of Mali was overrun and annexed as a vassal state of Sumanguru Kante, ruler of the powerful neighboring kingdom of Sosso. This was reported to have been inspired by the Sosso king's desire to possess the great gold mines at a city called Boure (or Bitu) within the borders of Mali.

Tradition relates that Sumanguru ordered the death of 11 sons of Nare Famanga, then king of Mali. One son who Sumanguru thought he could make into a puppet ruler was spared. This son was Sundiata, also known as Mari of Jata. Sundiata was a physical weakling and nothing by way of opposition was expected of him. Sundiata's health improved as he grew older and, as his strength increased, he resolved to free Mali from the domination of the Sosso, and to seek revenge against Sumanguru for the assassination of his brothers. Aided by an uncle, Prince Danguina-Konte, and other princes of Mali, Sundiata raised a large army. They marched against Sumanguru, met, and defeated him. After they killed him in the great battle at Kerina not far from the Niger, in 1235, they annexed the Kingdom of Sosso as a dependency of Mali.

Sundiata's able administration rendered prosperous not only domains under his rule but those bordering his empire as well. The rich products of his land, and the safety and security that he guaranteed to all, attracted merchants and traders from distant places. The far-flung renown of his armies caused the rights and property of his subjects to be well respected wherever his nationals traveled in neighboring lands. As a result of these activities and developments, Mali was transformed during the reign of Sundiata from an obscure and relatively small kingdom into a large and powerful empire that was to remain the most influential state in Western Africa for more than two centuries.

"Sundiata's able administration rendered prosperous not only domains under his rule but those bordering his empire as well."

In 1285 A.D. Sukura seized the throne. Some say he was a freed slave. Sukura, who was a general in the army at the time. He proved himself worthy of the position that he assumed. He continued the work and policies of his predecessor. Leading his army in person, he carried out successful campaigns in the north and west in the districts of Massinia and Jenne and against the Tucolors of Terkrur, and in the east he warred

39

against the Songhay in and around the city of Gao. The districts conquered in the western campaign were incorporated into the empire.

Sukura promoted commercial relations with the Muslim kingdoms of the Sahara and North Africa as far as Tripoli, Mauritania and Morocco, and he engaged in similar activities with kingdoms in the east and south. In his time, the empire was commercially prosperous. It was visited by traders and merchants from many distant African lands.

In the last year of the thirteenth century, Sukura made the pilgrimage to Mecca. He planned to return by the great southern pilgrim route rather than through Egypt, but, on reaching the coast of east Africa, he was assassinated near the port of Djibouti by a band of Danakiles "who [be]grudged him his gold." His companions embalmed his body and brought it back by way of Abyssinia, the eastern Sudan, and Wadai as far as Kuka in the kingdom of Bornu. Here the king of Bornu—presumably Mai Ibrahim (1288-1304 A.D.)—sent messengers to Mali to inform the court and the people of the misfortune that had overtaken their king.

An embassy was sent from Mali to Bornu to serve as an honorary escort of the late king's companions who were returning with the body. Sukura, though of lowly origin, was given the honor of a royal burial by the people and the nobility of Mali in testimony of their gratitude for the splendid service he had rendered the country.

According to Ibn Khaldun, Mansa Musa was the grandson of a sister of Sundiata. He is the best known of all the rulers of Mali and, with the possible exception of his great uncle, he is universally regarded as the greatest figure in the long line of princes that his royal family gave to the empire. Like Sundiata, Mansa Wali, and Sukuru, he extended the boundaries of his empire and actively promoted agriculture, industry and trade. It was, however, the celebrated pilgrimage that he made to the holy land in Arabia that contributed most to the great renown that was his in the larger world.

"According to Ibn Khaldun, Mansa Musa was the grandson of a sister of Sundiata. He is the best known of all the rulers of Mali."

This celebrated pilgrimage began in 1324 in the seventeenth year of his reign. References to this are preserved in the writings of several Muslim historians of the age, and all agree that it was the most colorful and spectacular mission of the king that had ever been made by any follower of the Prophet up to that time. It is safe to say that nothing equalling it has occurred since.

The royal caravan, according to some writers, included 12,000 persons, but other writers place the number at 60,000. Part of this great host was composed of a large military escort, and it is reported that there were thousands of attendants and servants. Among them were expert cooks whose duty was to prepare elaborate repasts for the king, his courtiers and their friends.

To provide for the expenses of the journey, Mansa Musa started out with gold worth $10 million today. This was carried, it is reported, on the backs of eighty camels, each bearing a load of three hundred—a total of twenty-four thousand pounds of pure gold. When the caravan was on the march, Mansa Musa was preceded by an escort of five hundred men on foot. These men were dressed in brocades and silks, and each carried a staff of gold weighing five hundred mitkales, or six pounds—a total of three thousand pounds of gold.

"To provide for the expenses of the journey, Mansa Musa started out with gold, which was carried, it is reported, on the backs of eighty camels, each bearing a load of three hundred—a total of twenty-four thousand pounds of pure gold."

Throughout the pilgrimage, the splendor of the caravan caused a great sensation in all the countries it passed through, and everyone marveled at the wealth and magnificence of the royal cortege. It is related that Mansa Musa gave twenty thousand gold pieces in alms at every town where he stopped. On Fridays he gave gold sufficient to build a mosque.

In Mecca, Mansa Musa met and formed a close relationship with Abu Ishak Ibrahim Es Saheli, a noted Moorish poet and architect from Granada in Spain. The emperor invited him to return with him to the Sudan. Es Saheli was appointed chief architect of the empire and erected numerous splendid buildings in various towns and cities of Mali.

In the holy cities of Arabia, Mansa Musa was particularly generous in his charitable gifts. In fact, it is said that because of his great generosity, the extensive financial preparations that he made for the journey proved inadequate, and that on his return to Cairo, he found it necessary to borrow a large amount of gold to enable him to keep up his customary benefactions. It is reported that the king had no difficulty in securing all the funds needed for this purpose, and that the loan was promptly repaid on his return to his native land.

While traveling in the desert, couriers met the caravan and informed Mansa Musa that in his absence his general and lieutenant Sagamandia, had attacked and captured Gao, capital of the neighboring Kingdom of Songhay. The emperor decided, therefore, to visit Gao and receive the homage of Za Soboi, the Songhay king. Thus, in 1325 A.D., Mansa made an impressive entry into the conquered city and received in person the submission of his new vassal.

To ensure his fidelity, Mansa Musa required that Za Soboi offer two of his sons as hostages. In compliance with this request, the princes, Ali Kolon and Suleiman Nare, were turned over to Mansa Musa, and when he left the city, they accompanied him to the capital of Mali. This act was of great importance in the subsequent history of both Mali and Songhay.

Mansa Musa died in 1332 A.D. after a 25-year reign. He left behind him an empire that was remarkable for its size and wealth. Moreover, Mansa Musa's empire provided a striking example of the African capacity for political organization. At the time of his death, the empire of Mali extended from Terkur, bordering on the Atlantic as far east as Takkedda—a distance of approximately 1500 miles. On the south, it extended to the powerful kingdoms of Ashanti and the Mossi, and according to Ibn Kaldun, a great but indefinite part of the Western Sahara in the north was a tributary to Mansa Musa's empire. Ahmed Baba, commenting upon the prowess of Mali in Mansa Musa's time, has said, "It possessed an aggressive strength without measure or limit." A noted modern writer declares that Mali at this period was "the vastest empire that ever existed in Africa and one of the most considerable that has ever existed in the whole world."

"Mansa Musa's empire provided a striking example of the African capacity for political organization."

Mansa Musa was succeeded by his son, Mansa Maghan, who reigned for four years. During his brief reign, two events greatly reduced the prestige and power of the empire of Mali. In 1333, shortly after Maghan's ascension, Nassegue, the King of Morho Naba of Yatenga, one of the two powerful Mossi kingdoms situated in the bend of the Niger, invaded Mali from the south, marched on the city of Timbuktu, defeated the garrison

44

that had been stationed there by Mansa Maghan, and pillaged and burned a considerable part of the city.

The Mossi, unlike the peoples of Mali and Songhay, still adhered to the ancient native religion of West Africa, and their attack on Timbuktu initiated a series of conflicts between the Muslims and non-Muslim states that was to last for more than two hundred years. Although the king of Mossi made no attempt to hold Timbuktu and there was no loss of territory by Mali, his capture and the sacking of the city constituted a severe blow to the city's prestige.

The second event during Mansa Maghan's reign did, however, result in the loss of considerable territory. In 1335 A.D., Ali Kolon and Suleiman Nare, the two sons of Za Soboi, the vassal king of Songhay, escaped from the capital of Mali where they had been taken as hostages of Mansa Musa 10 years before. The king sent out swift detachments that overtook the fleeing hostages, but they fought so valiantly that they could not be recaptured. They succeeded in reaching their own land safely. Soon after his return, Ali Kolon, aided by his brother and supported by the people of Songhay, proclaimed himself king and successfully freed his kingdom from the dominion of Mali.

In 1352 the historian Ibn Battuta visited Mali. Beyond Walata (north of Ghana), he found an almost entirely African population. He described the roads as perfectly safe from Walata to Mali. Provisions such as milk, chickens, rice, flour, and beans were found everywhere, and as for drink the inhabitants had water mixed with flour and honey. In Timbuktu, the capital, there were numerous lawyers in a flourishing economy. The king (at that time, Suleiman) held audiences in a hall adorned with gold and silver plaques. Ibn Battuta relates how the chief of Walata, accused of robbing a merchant, had to come to Mali in person, where he was found guilty and disgraced by the king. Ibn Battuta considered the Mali people very just. Mali, at its height, was a jewel among West African nations.

> *"Ibn Battuta relates how the chief of Walata, accused of robbing a merchant, had to come to Mali in person, where he was found guilty and disgraced by the king."*

Songhay was the third of the great empires of Western Sudan. From the early part of the fourteenth century until the time of the Moorish invasion in 1591 A.D., Songhay's city of Timbuktu was the intellectual center of Africa. African scholars were enjoying a renaissance in Timbuktu at the University of Sankore, which was known and respected throughout most of Africa and in parts of Europe. In *Timbuktu the Mysterious*, Felix DuBois gives us a description of this center of learning:

> The scholars of Timbuktu yielded in nothing, to the saints in their sojourns in the foreign universities of Fez, Tunis, and Cairo. They astounded the most learned men of Islam by their erudition. That these Negroes were on a level with the Arabian savants is proved

by the fact that they were installed as professors in Morocco and Egypt. In contrast to this, we find that the Arabs were not always equal to the requirements of Sankore.

Felix DuBois introduces Ahmed Baba as one of the greatest African scholars of the late sixteenth century. The last chancellor of the University of Sankore, Baba, was a brilliant example of the range and depth of West African intellectual activity before the colonial era. Ahmed Baba was the author of more than forty books, each having a different theme. He was in Timbuktu when it was invaded by the Moroccans in 1592 A.D., and he was one of the first citizens to protest the occupation of his beloved hometown. Ahmed Baba was imprisoned and eventually exiled to Morocco. During his expatriation from Timbuktu, his collection of 1600 books, one of the richest libraries of his day, was lost.

"Ahmed Baba, during his expatriation from Timbuktu, lost his collection of 1600 books, which was one of the richest libraries of his day."

During the Moorish invasion, West Africa entered a period of decline. Wreck and ruin became the order of the day. When the Europeans arrived in this part of Africa and saw these conditions, they assumed that nothing of order and value had ever existed in these countries. This mistaken impression, too often repeated, has influenced the interpretation of African and African American life for over four hundred years.

47

The two-hundred year turning point in European and world history is from 1400 to 1600 A.D. During this period Europe began to recover from the lethargy of the Middle Ages. From Moorish Spain, which had been ruled by Arabs, Berbers, and Africans, Europeans relearned maritime skills through translations made by scholars. By 1450 A.D., Spain had recovered part of its territory and had begun to take advantage of the internal struggle between its invaders. While still a colony, Spain began to have colonial aspirations of its own. The Portuguese had already started the slave trade along the west coast of Africa. This trade did not flourish until a market was created for the slave trade. There was a great need for labor, and the market supplied the labor that was needed for the European expansion into what is referred to as the "New World."

The Africans, Arabs, and Berbers lost control of Spain and the Mediterranean in 1492 A.D. Africa's time of tragedy and decline started both in Europe and in Africa itself. While the New World's discovery was a happy occasion for Europe, it was a sad occasion for Africa.

The Atlantic slave trade

Most people look upon the African slave trade as though it were the only system of slavery known to man. Slavery is an old institution, and there are no people who have not at some time in history been a victim of it in one form or the other. The African slave trade can best be understood if we take a brief look at the historical roots of slavery as a world institution.

Slavery in ancient societies was appreciably different from the type of slavery that was introduced into Africa by Europeans in the fifteenth and sixteenth centuries. In most ancient societies the slave was held in servitude for a limited time, for specific reasons, and, in most cases, the slaves were captured in local wars. Skin color was not a factor as to whether a person did or did not become a slave. In most cases, the slave had some rights that the master had to respect. In ancient Egypt, Kush, Greece, and early Rome, there were clearly defined codes of conduct governing the relationship between the slaves and their masters. Some of the earliest of these codes are recorded in the laws of Moses.

In W.O. Blake's *The History of Slavery and the Slave Trade,* the character of early slavery is discussed:

"The tragic and distinguishing feature of the slave trade that was introduced by Europeans was that it sought to dehumanize the slave."

The Mosaic institutions were rather predicated upon the previous existence of slavery in the surrounding nations, than designed to establish it for the first time; and the provisions of the Jewish law upon this subject, effected changes and modifications which must have improved the condition of slaves among the particular people. There were various modes by which the Hebrew might sell himself; a father might sell his children; debtors might be delivered as slaves to their creditors; thieves who were unable to make restitution for the property stolen were sold for the benefit of the sufferers. Prisoners of war were subjected to servitude; and if a Hebrew captive was redeemed by another Hebrew from a Gentile, he might be sold to another Israelite. At the return of the year of jubilee all Jewish captives were set free. However, by some writers it is stated that this did not apply to foreign slaves held in bondage; as, over those, the master had entire control.

The law of Moses provides that "if a man smite his servant or his maid with a rod, and he dies under his hand he shall be surely punished." This restriction is said by some to have applied only to Hebrew slaves, and not to foreign captives who were owned by Jews. Mosaic laws declared the terms upon which a Hebrew, who had been sold, could redeem himself, or be redeemed by his friends, and his right to take with him his wife and children, when discharged from bondage.

The main point of this reference is that the slaves of the ancient world were treated with some humane consideration. This was not less true of ancient Asia and Africa. In fact, in Africa, in both ancient and modern times, slaves were known to rise above their servitude and become kings in the very houses in which they had been slaves. That slavery existed in West Africa prior to contact with Europeans is often used to justify the European slave trade. The two systems had few similarities.

"The apologia for the slave trade had already started in Europe with Europeans attempting to justify the enslavement of other Europeans."

The tragic and distinguishing feature of the slave trade that was introduced by Europeans was that it sought to dehumanize the slave. This dehumanization effort continued in many ways throughout the slavery period and well into the colonial era. This policy was given crucial support in part by the Christian church and was later extended by the writers of the seventeenth and eighteenth centuries. The myth that Africans had no history or culture comes out of this period.

The apologia for the slave trade had already started in Europe with Europeans attempting to justify the enslavement of other Europeans. This is a neglected aspect of European history. There was a concerted

53

effort to obtain European labor to open up the vast regions of the New World. In what became the United States, white enslavement started before Black enslavement. In a 1969 *Ebony Magazine* article entitled, "White Servitude in the United States," historian Lerone Bennett, Jr. discusses this period:

> When someone removes the cataracts of whiteness from our eyes, and when we look with unclouded vision on the bloody shadows of the American past, we will recognize for the first time that the African American, who was so often second in freedom, was also second in slavery. Indeed, it will be revealed that the African American was third in slavery. For he inherited his chains, in a manner of speaking, from the pioneer bondsmen, who were red and white.

The enslavement of both red and white men in the early American colonies was a contradiction of English law. The colonies were founded with the understanding that neither chattel slavery nor villenage would be recognized. Yet forced labor was widely used in England. This system was transferred to the colonies and used to justify a form of slavery that was visited upon red and white men. Concise information on this system and how it developed is revealed in Albert Bushnell Hart's *Slavery and Abolition, 1831-1841.*

An apprentice would serve his seven years, and take floggings as his master saw fit; a hired servant would carry out his contract for his term of service. Convicts of the state, often including political offenders, were slaves of the state and were sometimes sold to private owners overseas. The colonists claimed those rights over some of their white fellow countrymen.

There was a large class of "redemptioners" who had agreed that their service should be sold for a brief term of years to pay their passage money. "Indentured" or "indented" servants, bought by their masters under legal obligation, served even longer terms, subject to the same penalties of branding, whipping, and mutilation as African slaves. These forms of servitude were supposed to be limited in duration and transmitted no claim to the servant's children. In spite of this servitude, the presumption in law was that a white man was born free.

Slavery and resistance in South America and the Caribbean

Africans and Europeans were part of a world drama of the most massive movement of people in human history. *In Slave and Citizen: The*

Negro in the Americas, the author, Frank Tannenbaum, has described this event:

> The settling of the Western hemisphere by people coming from Europe and Africa was an adventure on a grand scale, involving diverse people, varying cultures, millions of human beings, and hundreds of years. The common element was the new world, though strangely dissimilar in physical features and cultural type. But the student discerns many an analogous design, patterned by the newcomers as they established themselves in the strange and unexplored regions.

Africans were brought into South America and the Caribbean islands to replace Indians as a labor force. Under the impact of the European presence, the Indians died and were killed in large numbers. In the first one hundred years after European settlement, most of the Indians in the Caribbean Islands had died out and the Indian population of South America had drastically declined.

The bitter international rivalry over colonial possessions and spheres of influence in the slave trade had placed Africans in the crossfire between competing European powers. The Papal Bull of 1455 AD had authorized the Portuguese and the Spanish to "reduce to servitude all infidel people." Because most Europeans in the slave trade labeled African people as infidels, people without culture, and outside of humanity, they were mentally unprepared to deal with African culture as a factor in the revolts against slavery and oppression. Slavery was a moral and philosophical problem to the Europeans. They wanted to present themselves to the world as Christians, but they also wanted to continue in the business of slavery, which was inhumane and anti-Christian.

The spread of the plantation system in the Americas and in the Caribbean required more African labor. Slaves were bought in large numbers and generally kept together. Some of the plantation owners thought that in this way the Africans could communicate with each other and more work could be accomplished. They did not seem to realize that communication is the best way to perpetuate a people's culture. With the drums and a common language that most of the Africans understood because they came from the same general area within Africa, communication systems were developed that would later serve to facilitate slave revolts.

"The plantation system was a natural incubator for slave revolts."

The plantation system was a natural incubator for slave revolts. In many ways, the plantations were small semiautonomous states. The plantation owners and their overseers had complete authority over the lives of the Africans. Very often their attempt to break the spirit of the Africans set rebellion in motion. The newly arrived Africans were the most effective in these early slave revolts. They were closer to their African culture and had not adjusted to slavery.

The planters' search for a way to keep down uprisings created another dilemma. To let the Africans keep their own religion and way of life was to facilitate the uprisings, and to convert them to Christianity would make them turn against slavery as their Christian duty. The dilemma of how to control the slaves marked each period of slavery and the slave trade and continued into the first half of the nineteenth century. The inequities of slavery forced the Africans to take refuge in mountains and in woods where African cultural continuity played a major role in holding bands of runaway slaves together and in planning strategies for their survival.

"...African cultural continuity played a major role in holding bands of runaway slaves together and in planning strategies for their survival."

The Spaniards called the fugitive slaves *Cimarrones,* and the French adopted the word to their language and called them *Maroons.* Flight was the slaves' goal, because it meant liberty, however temporary. In the jungles and virgin forests, protected by the lush tropical growth, some of these Africans developed self-contained communities and for years avoided reenslavement. Sometimes, according to Fernando Ortiz, in *Los Negros Esclaves* (Black Slaves), fugitive slaves settled in hidden spots such as mountains—where the access was difficult—became strong, and lived independent lives. Sometimes they were successful in developing farms similar to those they had known in Africa. The slaves in this state of rebellion were called *Apalencados* and their retreats were called *Palenques*.

Perhaps the first recorded Black slave insurrection took place in Santo Domingo on December 26, 1522 in the sugar mill of Don Diego Colon, who was the Admiral and Governor of the area. Although the rebels fought valiantly, they were subdued. Those who survived were hanged. In 1529, Black mutineer slaves destroyed Santa Marta. Slaves continuously protested in Panama in 1531. Frightened by the number of rebellious Africans, European settlers slaughtered Africans in Mexico in 1537. The settlers simply quartered a few dozen whom they suspected of thinking of rebelling. Indians and Africans rebelled against slavery during the first days of European conquest and colonization of the Island of Cuba. In 1533, Governor Manuel De Rojas sent two squads to the mines of Jababo in the province of Cueyba to subdue four Africans who had hidden there. These Africans fought to their death.

The revolt of the Maroons, both in Jamaica and in Suriname, helped to create the condition and attitude that made the Berbice revolt in Guiana possible. These revolts collectively helped to create the condition and attitude that went into the making of the most successful slave revolt in history, the Haitian Revolution. This revolt was brought into being by three of the most arresting personalities in Caribbean history—Toussaint L'Ouverture, Jacques Dessalines and Henri Christophe. The distinguishing aspect of this revolution is that it achieved what the others were not able to achieve—nationhood.

The slaves in Jamaica fought longer and harder than the slaves in Haiti, but they did not achieve nationhood because they fought under different political circumstances. The news of these revolts reached the United States, partly through slave sailors on ships between the Caribbean, South America, and the United States. This was part of the stimulus that helped to set in motion the massive slave revolts in the United States in the early nineteenth century.

Slavery and resistance in the United States

The presence of African people as slaves played a major role in the United States in the years between their arrival in Jamestown, Virginia in 1619 and the period of the American Revolution in 1776. Revolts and a struggle for manhood, womanhood, and dignity continued throughout this period until the eve of the Civil War when the nature of this struggle took a different form.

The new nature of this struggle is best reflected in the lives of eminent African American personalities in the first half of the nineteenth century. Referring to some of the leaders, their organizations, and objectives, Dorothy Porter observes:

> The pioneer colonization projects of Paul Cuffe and Daniel Coker in Sierra Leone reflect the African American's world view of race and of race destiny for the Blacks as they established communities overseas. Many African Americans had significant connections with African, Haitian, and other Black communities abroad. The stimulus of the British antislavery movement served to enhance African American prospects for emigration to lands where their people might be free.

While Paul Cuffe's ideas for African colonization had been expressed in his writing during the closing years of the eighteenth century, he did not succeed in taking any African Americans back to Africa until the early part of the nineteenth century. Thirty-eight Black settlers arrived with Paul Cuffe when he landed his ship, the *Traveller*, in Freetown, Sierra Leone, on the morning of 3 February 1816. In many ways this was the beginning of the African colonization movement. The back-to-Africa idea, and Africa as a subject for African American writers, continued throughout the nineteenth century and reemerged in the twentieth century. Paul Cuffe was one of the paramount figures who helped to give birth to this idea.

The Free African Society was organized by the Black Methodists in 1787. This society under the leadership of Richard Allen and Absalom Jones brought into being the independent Black church in the United States—the African Methodist Episcopal Church. The early Black churches were more than religious organizations. They performed the services of social agencies, publishers, community centers, and, occasionally, hiding places for escaped slaves. The first historical protest and literary writings of the Black freedmen in the New England states found an outlet in the church or organizations affiliated with the church.

"The early Black churches were more than religious organizations. They performed the services of social agencies, publishers, community centers, and, occasionally, hiding places for escaped slaves."

Pamphlets, broadsheets, and monographs continued to appear throughout the first half of the nineteenth century. Writers used this medium to express the difficulties Blacks experienced in seeking freedom, and their appreciation to the people of the city of Salem, Massachusetts for showing signs of support for African "freedom." These writers would help to establish the early Black press in the United States. Some of them became editors of such papers as *Freedom's Journal*, *The North Star*, and the *Anglo-African Magazine*.

The subject of colonization and migration to Africa was debated in the pages of these publications. Many Blacks who were sure about Africa being the homeland of their people were not sure about returning to Africa. Others saw the return to Africa as the only solution to their problems. The plans of the American Colonization Society, strongly influenced by whites, included returning only free Blacks to Africa. The Black press mainly saw this as an attempt to protect the institution of slavery by removing a very active abolitionist group. This insight into a then prevailing situation did not deny their deep cultural ties to Africa. The colonization movement, literally started by Paul Cuffe, continued, concurrent with the fight for African people to enjoy complete citizenship status in the United States.

The spiritual and cultural return to Africa is reflected in the names of early Black institutions, especially in the churches. In, *The Redemption of Africa and Black Religion,* St. Clair Drake sketches this picture of the Black church during its formative years:

> Black people under slavery turned to the Bible to "prove" that Black people, Ethiopians, were powerful and respected when white men in Europe were barbarians. Ethiopia came to symbolize all of Africa; and throughout the nineteenth century, the redemption of Africa became one important focus of meaningful activity for leaders among new world Africans. "Ethiopianism" became the

energizing myth in both the new world and in African itself for those pre-political movements that arose while the powerless were gathering their strength for realistic and rewarding political activity. Its force is now almost spent, but "Ethiopianism" left an enduring legacy to the people who fought for Black power in the twentieth century, and some of its development needs to be understood.

Black churches sprang up wherever Black people lived: The First African Baptist Church, Savannah, Georgia (1788); African Baptist Church, Lexington, Kentucky (1790); Abyssinia Baptist Church, New York (1800); The Free African Meeting House, Boston, Massachusetts (1805); The First African Baptist Presbyterian Church, Philadelphia, Pennsylvania (1809); The Union Church of Africans, Wilmington, Delaware (1813); The First African Baptist Church, New Orleans, Louisiana (1826); The African Methodist Episcopal Church, Philadelphia, Pennsylvania (1816); The First African Baptist Church, Richmond, Virginia (1841). These institutions and their congregations kept alive the African connection. Some Blacks, independent of the American Colonization Society, went back to Africa to preach, teach, and live out the rest of their lives.

The vision of Africa that began to develop during the eighteenth century was enhanced by organizations using the word, "Africa" or "African," in referring to their objectives. While they addressed themselves mainly to the plight of African people in the United States, they emphasized that they belonged to a universal people, with land, history, and culture. This, of course, did not settle the matter. According to W.E.B. Du Bois, free Blacks strongly advocated a return to Africa. Their agitation had much to do with uncertainty about their status as freed men in a slaveholding society.

Thus the back-to-Africa ideal had already been a recurring theme in African American life and thought for more than a generation. This idea was strong during the formative years of the American Colonization Society and succeeded in convincing some of the most outstanding Black men of the eighteenth and nineteenth centuries, such as John Russwurm, editor of *Freedom's Journal,* and Lott Carey, the powerful Virginia preacher. Other men were against the program of the American Colonization Society and were equally outstanding, such as Frederick Douglass. Some contended that it was a philanthropic enterprise; others considered it a scheme for getting rid of the free people of color because of their seeming menace to slavery.

In the year 1829, two events occurred that brought radical change and much debate to the Black movement in the United States. John B. Russwurm abandoned his opposition to the American Colonization Society and announced that he had been converted "to the view that the free Negro could help himself and his race best by giving strong support to Liberia." The establishment of this state on the West Coast of Africa was a historical turning point in the African Americans' attempt to return in body as well as in mind to their African homeland.

In Liberia, John B. Russwurm moved to a position that today would be called Black nationalism. He established another newspaper, the *Liberia Herald,* and served as superintendent of schools. He further distinguished himself as Governor of the Colony of Cape Palmas, which was established in Liberia by the Maryland Colonization Society.

The other event was the publication of a document in September 1829, now best known as David Walker's *Appeal.* (The third and final edition was published in 1830.) As a result of *Walker's Appeal,* the debate over the destiny of African Americans was lifted to a new level of consciousness. It has been said that if any single event may be said to have triggered the Black revolt, it was the publication of *David Walker's Appeal to the Coloured Citizens of the World.* The slaveholding South saw in it only incitement to rebellion, and went to great lengths to suppress it. Even in the North, where the abolition of slavery had not yet taken root, there was agreement that the pamphlet was inappropriate and incendiary. With the appearance of the *Appeal,* a more militant fight against slavery was born. In calling for the slaves to take up arms against their masters, Walker went beyond nationalism and saw slavery as a crisis affecting African people everywhere.

In the years between 1830 and 1850, the debate over the plans of the American Colonization Society continued. The society was still white-dominated and held in suspicion by a large number of African Americans. In *Pan-Negro Nationalism in the World Before 1862*, Hollis R. Lynch has pointed out why men like Paul Cuffe and John B. Russwurm gave their support to the American Colonization Society despite having some misgivings about some aspects of its program. "Whatever the motive of the Society's leaders and supporters," Lynch has said, "the Society was creating a Negro state in Africa."

"Walker went beyond nationalism and saw slavery as a crisis affecting African people everywhere."

In 1851, John B. Russwurm died in Liberia, and in the same year Edward Wilmot Blyden went to Africa and established himself in Liberia. He was destined to become the greatest Black intellectual of the nineteenth century. He concerned himself with the plight of African people the world over, and eventually built a bridge of understanding between the people of African origin in the West Indies, the United States, and Africa. More than anyone else in the nineteenth century, and the early part of the twentieth century, Edward W. Blyden called upon the Black man to reclaim himself and his ancient African glory. The concept now called Negritude, started with Edward W. Blyden.

In the decade before the Civil War, a new renaissance of interest in Africa by African Americans was reflected in the Black press and in the speeches of a growing number of Black men of affairs, particularly Martin R. Delany. Delany was proud of his African background and of the Mandingo blood that flowed in his veins. He was one of the leaders of the great debate following the passage of the Fugitive Slave Act of 1850. He was the spokesman for Black people who felt that the bitter climate in America had made life unbearable for them. Delany was the strongest voice in several conventions of free Blacks to discuss plans for emigrating to Africa. In 1859, he led the first and only exploratory part of American-born Africans to the land of their forefathers. In the region of the Niger River, in the area that is now Nigeria, Delany's party carried out scientific studies and made agreements with several African kings for the settlement of emigrants from America.

Martin Delany was accompanied on this expedition by Robert Campbell, a Jamaican, who had been director of the scientific department of the Institute for Colored Youth in Philadelphia, and a member of the International Statistical Congress in London. His account of the expedition can be found in his book, *A Pilgrimage To My Motherland, An Account of a Journey Among the Egbas and Yorubas of Central Africa in 1859-1860.* About his report, Robert Campbell has said:

> After what is written in the context, if I am still asked what I think of Africa for a Colored man to live and do well in, I simply answer, that with as good prospects in America as colored men have generally, I have determined with my wife and children to go to Africa to live, leaving the inquirer to interpret the reply for himself.

"What needs to be remembered about this mid-nineteenth century back-to-Africa movement is that, to a moderate degree, it was successful."

What needs to be remembered about this mid-nineteenth century back-to-Africa movement is that, to a moderate degree, it was successful. There was, of course, no mass exodus to Africa. Individual families did go to Africa at regular intervals for the next fifty years. In a biography by Dorothy Sterling, Martin Delany is referred to as "The father of Black Nationalism." Martin Delany was a multitalented freedom fighter who seemed to have crammed a half dozen lifetimes into one. He was a dentist, an explorer, a scientist, a soldier, and a politician. He was a renaissance man of his day, and if he were alive today he would still be considered the same.

Martin R. Delany was coeditor with Frederick Douglass of *The North Star*. In Delany's own time, he was a famous figure and widely known for his lectures and his association with John Brown and others. Before the Civil War, he advocated the establishment of a state by African Americans in the Niger Valley (in present-day Nigeria). This interest in

Africa was continued under the leadership of men like Reverend Alexander Crummell, and Bishop Henry McNeal Turner.

General interest in Africa continued through the pre-Civil War years although emigration efforts to establish an autonomous nation for African Americans did not succeed. The Civil War and the promises to African Americans that followed lessened some of the interest in Africa. Pap Singleton started an internal settlement scheme to settle Blacks in the unused areas of America, mainly, at this time, the state of Kansas. He hoped to establish free separate Black communities.

The betrayal of Reconstruction and increased lynchings and other atrocities against African Americans made a new generation of Black thinkers and freedom fighters once again turn to Africa. New men and movements entered the area of struggle. The most notable of the new personalities was Bishop Henry McNeal Turner. In *Black Exodus*, Edwin S. Redkey gives this view of Bishop Turner's importance to the history of this period:

> Bishop Henry McNeal Turner was, without a doubt, the most prominent and outspoken American advocate of Black emigration in the years between the Civil War and the first World War. By constant agitation he kept African Americans aware of their African heritage and their disabilities in the United States. Turner possessed a dominating personality, a biting tongue, and a pungent vocabulary

which gained him high office and wide audiences, first in Georgia's Reconstruction politics and later in the African Methodist Episcopal (AME) Church. In his bitter disappointment with the American treatment of Blacks, the Bishop had an all-consuming Nationalism which demanded emigration to Africa. To understand this forceful agitation in the years following 1890, one must know Turner's background and the nature of his vision of Africa.

African Americans in the twentieth century

African Americans entered the twentieth century searching for a new direction, politically, culturally, and institutionally. New men and movements were emerging. The Niagara Movement, under the leadership of W.E.B. Du Bois and Monroe Trotter, was born in 1905. Some of the ideas of the Niagara Movement went into the making of the NAACP in 1909. Black interest in Africa continued but was abated by the burden of the troubles at home. The end of the First World War brought no improvement to the lives of African Americans. Prevailing conditions made a large number of them ripe for the militant Africa-oriented program of Marcus Garvey.

In the appendix to the second edition of his book, *Black Jacobins,* the Caribbean scholar C.L.R. James observes that two West Indians "using the ink of Negritude [,] wrote their names, imperishably on the front pages of the history of our times." James is referring to Aime Cesaire and Marcus Garvey. He places Marcus Garvey at the forefront of the group of twentieth century Black radicals whose ideas and programs still reverberate within present-day liberation movements. Marcus Garvey was a man of his time who, in retrospect, was ahead of his time. His ideas have since resurfaced and are being seriously reconsidered as a major factor in the liberation of African people the world over.

James further reminds us that Marcus Garvey, an immigrant from Jamaica, was the only Black man who succeeded in building a mass movement among African Americans. He advocated the return of Africa to the Africans and people of African descent. He organized, maybe too hurriedly and with a shortage of competently trained people, the institutions and enterprises that would make this possible. His movement began to develop an international framework around 1921.

"Marcus Garvey was a man of his time who, in retrospect, was ahead of his time. His ideas have since resurfaced and are being seriously reconsidered as a major factor in the liberation of African people the world over."

In the 1920s the structure of the movement was shaken by internal strife and power-hungry personalities fighting for control. This infighting was part of what led to the arrest, trial, and subsequent deportation of Marcus Garvey. C.L.R. James nevertheless summarized his achievements:

> But Garvey managed to convey to Negroes everywhere (and to the rest of the world) his passionate belief that Africa was the home of a civilization which had once been great and would be great again. When you bear in mind the slenderness of his resources, the vast material forces and the prevailing social conceptions which auto-

matically sought to destroy him, his achievement remains one of the propagandistic miracles of this century.

After the deportation of Marcus Garvey and the beginning of the Great Depression, interest in Garvey and the back-to-Africa idea waned and was not rekindled until the Italian-Ethiopian War (1935-1936). This war and its implications for African people at home and abroad stirred latent African consciousness in the African communities in the West. The Blyden Society, The Ethiopian World Federation, and other organizations attracted a number of African supporters, some of whom were beyond the headlines, and predicted the future repercussions of Ethiopia's betrayal. Their press reports were a highwater mark in Black journalism.

"After the Second World War, African conciousness was reflected in the literature and activities of the Civil Rights Movement."

A number of study groups showed interest in African history; the best known was the Blyden Society, named after the great nationalist, and benefactor of West Africa, Edward W. Blyden. During this period, the streets of Harlem were open forums, presided over by master speakers like Arthur Reed and his protege, Ira Kemp. Young Carlos Cook, founder of the Garvey-oriented African Pioneer Movement, was also on the scene bringing a nightly message to the community—a part of which was about Africa.

After the Second World War, African consciousness was reflected in the literature and activities of the Civil Rights Movement. Black newspapers began to pay more attention to items about the developing crisis in Africa concurrent with their interest in personalities like Martin Luther King, Jr. The coverage of news about Africa accelerated with the rise of the independence movement on the continent of Africa and reached a culmination in March 1957, when the Gold Coast gained its independence and took the ancient name of Ghana. Kwame Nkrumah, the first prime minister of Ghana, became a national hero to African Americans. Thus, the African freedom explosion was set in motion.

"Toward the close of the 1960's many African Americans became disillusioned by white resistance to equal rights for African Americans."

This was an international movement affecting African people everywhere. The antecedents of this movement were the nineteenth century struggles against slavery and oppression in Africa, the Americas, and the Caribbean islands. At the end of the nineteenth century and the beginning of the twentieth century, someone found a name for this struggle: *Pan-Africanism*. This movement contributed to the African independence explosion, the Caribbean movement for independence and federation, and the Civil Rights Movement for complete citizenship in the United States.

Toward the close of the 1960s, many African Americans became disillusioned by white resistance to equal rights for African Americans. They began to shift their attention away from protest-oriented approaches to militant approaches to racial equality in the United States. The era of the Black Revolution emerged as numerous groups advocating militarism, separatism, and cultural nationalism.

Huey P. Newton and Bobby Seale organized the Black Panther Party for Self-Defense, which called for "full employment, decent housing, Black control of the Black community, and an end to every form of repression and police brutality." Some African Americans felt that whites would never concede to racial equality, and that the creation of an independent Black state was the solution to resolving racial inequality. In 1967, the Black Power Conference in Newark, New Jersey; called for dividing the United States into two independent nations, one for whites, the other for Blacks.

Other African Americans focused on Africa as their home, and adopted African names and dress to express their connection with "the motherland." As Black nationalists, they demanded control of all institutions in the Black community, particularly the schools, colleges, and universities. Black nationalists insisted on introducing Black students to Black history, Black literature, and other subjects in Black studies.

The late sixties and the early seventies is also identified as the era of a Black political revolution. The number of Black representatives in state legislatures and Congress grew two- and three-fold- respectively. In 1966, there was no Black mayor in any American city. However, by 1973 African Americans served as mayors in several large cities nationwide, as well as in several small southern towns.

"The late sixties and the early seventies is also identified as the era of a Black political revolution.The number of Black representatives in the state legislatures and Congress grew two and three-fold respectively."

Some African Americans were not certain that they could achieve their goals through the established political organizations, or that the established political parties would take them seriously. These sentiments led to the calling of the first National Black Political Convention, which met in Gary, Indiana, in March 1972. Despite major opposition among delegates on policy issues, a committee of leaders released the National Black Political Agenda in May 1972. This agenda contained a poor people's platform, model pledges for political candidates seeking convention support, a bill for voter registration, and a bill for community self-determination.

In the August 1980 meeting, convention delegates passed a resolution to establish a national independent Black political party within one hundred days. The National Black Independent Political Party was founded in Philadelphia in November 1980, and its first party congress convened in August 1981.

By the middle seventies, the growth in Black political power and its rewards were considerable, but not great enough. Although African Americans won elective offices and received government appointments that they could only aspire to hold only two decades earlier, the number of Blacks holding elective and appointive offices was infinitesimal compared with Whites.

"By the middle seventies, the growth in Black political power and its rewards were considerable, but not great enough."

The economic disadvantages of African Americans persisted. So many Black families were unemployed and on welfare during the decade of the seventies that University of Chicago sociologist William Julius Wilson feared that the legacy of discrimination and oppression coupled with the technological revolution had created a permanent class of Black unskilled workers.

The Black middle class was undoubtedly growing in size and influence, but a huge economic gap existed between them and the white middle class. African Americans who occupied the middle class typically earned less, and had less opportunities for job advancement than their white counterparts.

African Americans sought economic power and became convinced that the ballot would help them secure it. Jesse Jackson announced his candidacy for president in October 1983. The American public had witnessed an African American making a formal bid for the presidency within a major political party only once before— Shirley Chisholm in 1972.

Jackson clearly stated that one of his main goals was to encourage the disfranchised to register and vote. People of all races and creeds rallied within his Rainbow Coalition for a common purpose: "to place men and women in the public service whose primary purpose was to serve the best interests of their constituents." Jackson's candidacies were undoubtedly a great stimulus to Black registration and voting and to the growth in Black officeholders. More African Americans voted in the presidential elections in 1984 and 1988 than ever before.

African Americans viewed their fate as inextricably linked to the fate of Africans throughout the world. In 1984, African Americans took the lead in pressuring the United States government to oppose apartheid in South Africa. African National Congress leader Nelson Mandela directed the attention of African Americans to Africa in a way that had not been done since the emergence of Kwame Nkrumah in Ghana in 1957. The political activities of Nelson Mandela's wife, Winnie Mandela, were equally influential. African Americans regarded her as the Pan-African nationalist who more directly linked the struggle against political and economic oppression in South Africa with the struggle for freedom for African people everywhere in the world.

Led by Randall Robinson, Mary Frances Berry, Eleanor Holmes Norton, Walter Fauntroy, Sylvia Hill and others. African Americans

"African Americans relentlessly held sit-in campaigns and pressured Congress to impose economic sanctions against the South African government."

relentlessly held sit-in campaigns and pressured Congress to impose economic sanctions against the South African government. Such activism assured that world opinion regarding apartheid was aroused, which helped speed the release of Nelson Mandela in February 1990. In the final years of the twentieth century, African Americans remain committed to continuing the struggle for freedom at home and abroad. The next logical step will involve African people everywhere building a world union and a new humanity.

Notes for further reading

To fully understand the role of African people in world history, it is essential that we take a holistic view of Africa's influence and examine the impact of African migrations throughout the world. Because elements of African culture and the presence of African people have been identified in regions outside of Africa, Africans apparently have had a curiosity about the lands beyond their continent over and above the curiosity they seem to have right now.

Sixteen small island nations in the Pacific have a population that appears to be indistinguishable from Africans in other parts of the world. How and when did they get there? What caused their migration to this region, which is so far from their original home in Africa? Their history is intriguing.

The original population of aborigines in Australia is basically African in appearance with a slightly Polynesian admixture. On the island nearby, the Tasmanians, who were destroyed in an act of genocide that the world has chosen to forget, were even more African in appearance.

The migration of Africans to lands beyond the shores of their continent began to occur over a thousand years before the beginning of the Arab slave trade in East Africa and the Atlantic slave trade in West Africa. This process occurred without any wars of consequence between the Africans and the people they visited in other lands. It is important to understand that racism has not always existed among humans. This phenomenon began in the fifteenth and sixteenth centuries during the rise of the Atlantic slave trade and subsequently colonialism.

Some old and new writings on the African presence abroad need to be thoroughly examined. In his two-volume work, *Anacalypsis*, Sir Godfrey Higgins alludes to the dispersion of Africans throughout the early ancient world, including the African presence in Asia and in early Europe. Higgins also emphasizes the significant contributions Africans made to the development of religions and cultures outside of Africa. Professor Joseph Harris's work, *The African Presence in Asia*, documents the early African presence in India. Other documentation of the African presence abroad include the "African Presence in Early Asia" and the "African Presence in Early Europe" in the *Journal of African Civilizations*, edited by Professor Ivan Van Sertima (vol. 7, no. 1 [April 1985], and vol. 7, no. 2 [November 1985] respectively). A comparatively recent work, *Dalit: The Black Untouchables of India* by V.T. Rajshekar, should be examined in order to understand the status of people of African descent in India today.

The important point to learn from these references is that Africans journeyed far beyond Africa during an early period in their history, and merged their cultures, languages, and technical know-how with others without ever declaring a war against any group. Africans left Africa with their humanity intact and respected the humanity of other people in their journeys abroad. This is an important lesson to understand today and apply in the future.

It is unfortunate that so much of the information on the world position of African people and the contributions they have made toward civilization have been lost from the history of mankind. In my opinion, the restoration of Africa's history is essential to the restoration of the African continent.

It is important that African people understand that African civilizations were well established before the political and intellectual emergence of Europe became a factor in world affairs. Most of the world's major religions and nearly every textbook have made a serious efforts to interpret history without Africans playing a major role. The fact that civilization started with African people has been ignored, and the contributions that African people are now making to the world are minimized.

To understand Africa's world position, one needs to look at the past and present, in order to prophesy what the future can be. It is my hope that this lecture, and the bibliography that follows, highlight some of the major contributions African people have made to world history and to humanity.

John Henrik Clarke , Professor Emeritus
African and World History
Department of Puerto Rican Studies
Hunter College

Select bibliography

ben-Jochannan, Yosef A.A.. *Africa, Mother of Western Civilization.* 1971* Baltimore: Black Classic Press, 1988.

_____. *Abu Simbel to Ghizeh: A Guide Book and Manual.* 1987* Baltimore: Black Classic Press, 1989.

_____. *Black Man of the Nile and His Family.* 1972* Baltimore: Black Classic Press, 1989.

_____. *The African Origins of Major Western Religions.* 1970* Baltimore: Black Classic Press, 1991.

Bennett, Lerone, Jr. *Before the Mayflower: A History of Black America.* Baltimore: Penguin Books, 1962.

_____."Birth of Black America." Part II: "White Servitude in America." *Ebony* 25 (November 1969): 31-34.

Blake, W.O. *The History of Slavery and the Slave Trade.* Columbus, Ohio: J.H. Miller, 1858.

Budge, Ernest A. *The Egyptian Book of the Dead.* London: British Museum, Longmans and Co., 1895.

Campbell, Robert. *A Pilgrimage To My Motherland, An Account of a Journey Among the Egbas and Yorubas of Central Africa in 1859-1860.* New York: Thomas Hamilton, 1861.

Clarke, John Henrik. *Africans at the Crossroads: Notes for an African World Revolution.* Trenton: Africa World Press, Inc., 1991.

_____, ed. *New Dimensions in African History: The London Lectures of Dr. Yosef ben-Jochannan and Dr. Henrik Clarke.* Trenton: Africa World Press, Inc., 1991.

Davidson, Basil. *A Guide to African History.* London: G. Allen and Unwin, [1963].

deGraft-Johnson, J.C. *African Glory.* 1954* Baltimore: Black Classic Press, 1986.

Delafosse, Maurice. *Negroes of Africa.* Washington, D.C.: The Associated Publishers, 1931.

Diop, Cheikh Anta. *African Origins of Civilization: Myth or Reality?* Westport, CT: Lawrence Hill & Co., 1974.

Drake, St. Clair. *The Redemption of Africa and Black Religion.* Chicago: Third World Press, 1974.

Dubois, Felix. *Timbuktoo the Mysterious. 1896** Westport, CT: Negro University Press. 1969.

Essien-Udom, E.U. *Black Nationalism: A Search for an Identity in America.* University of Chicago, 1965.

Franklin, John Hope. *From Slavery to Freedom: A History of Negro Americans. 1947** New York: Knopf, 1980.

Hall, Gwendolyn Midlo. *Social Control in Slave Plantation Societies. Baltimore: Johns Hopkins, 1972.*

Harris, Joseph E., ed. *Pillars in Ethiopian History. The William Leo Hansberry African History Notebook.* Vol. 1. Washington, D.C.: Howard University Press, 1974.

Hart, Albert Bushnell. *Slavery and Abolition, 1831-1841.* New Jersey: Harper and Brothers, 1906.

Jackson, John G. *Introduction to African Civilization.* Secaucus, NJ: Citadel Press, 1974.

James, C.L.R. *The Black Jacobins: Toussaint L'Ouverture & the San Domingo Revolution.* New York: Random, 1963.

Lane-Poole, Stanley. *The Story of the Moors in Spain.* 1886* Baltimore: Black Classic Press, 1990.

Leakey, L.S.B. *The Progress and Evolution of Man in Africa.* New York: Oxford, 1961.

Lynch, Hollis R. "Pan-Negro Nationalism in the New World, before 1862." In *The Making of Black America.* Edited by August Meier and Elliott Rudwick. Vol. 1. New York: Atheneum, 1969.

Massey, Gerald. *Ancient Egypt, The Light of the World.* 2 vols. 1907* Baltimore: Black Classic Press, 1992.

Moore, Richard B. *The Name Negro: Its Origin and Evil Use.* 1960* Baltimore: Black Classic Press, 1992.

_____. "The Significance of African History." *Amsterdam News.* August 12, 1967.

Oliver, Roland & Fage, J.D. *A Short History of Africa.* Baltimore: Penguin Books, [1962].

Ortiz, Fernando. *Los Negros Esclaves*. Habana: Revista Bimestre Cubana, 1916.

Porter, Dorothy., ed. *Negro Protest Pamphlets*, New York: Arno, 1969.

Rawlinson, George, ed. *The History of Herodotus*. 4 vols. New York: D. Appleton & Co., 1860.

Redkey, Edwin S. *Black Exodus: Black Nationalists and the Back-to-Africa Movements, 1890-1910*. New Haven: Yale University, 1969.

Rodney, Walter. *How Europe Underdeveloped Africa*. Washington, D.C.: Howard University Press, 1974.

Rogers, J.A. *World's Great Men of Color*. 1946-47* 2 vols. New York: Macmillan, 1972.

Sterling, Dorothy. *The Making of an Afro-American: Martin Robinson Delany*. Garden City, New York: Doubleday, 1971.

Tannebaum, Frank. *Slave and Citizen: The Negro in the Americas*. New York: Knopf, 1947.

Uya, Okon Edet. *Black Brotherhood, Afro-Americans and Africa*. Lexington, MA: D.C. Heath, [1970, 1971].

Walker, David. *Walker's Appeal. 1830**Baltimore: Black Classic Press, *1993.*

Williams, Bruce. "The Lost Pharaohs of Nubia." *Journal of African Civilizations* 6, no. 2 (November 1984): pp. 29-43.

Williams, Chancellor. *The Destruction of Black Civilization.* Chicago: Third World Press, 1974.

Williams, Eric. *Capitalism and Slavery.* New York: Capricorn Books, 1966.

*Indicates first year published.